2024 VISION BOARD Clip Art Book

Work & Business | Home
Healthy Eating | Family

© COPYRIGHT 2023 - ALL RIGHTS RESERVED.

YOU MAY NOT REPRODUCE, DUPLICATE OR SEND THE CONTENTS OF THIS BOOK WITHOUT DIRECT WRITTEN PERMISSION FROM THE AUTHOR. YOU CANNOT HEREBY DESPITE ANY CIRCUMSTANCE BLAME THE PUBLISHER OR HOLD HIM OR HER TO LEGAL RESPONSIBILITY FOR ANY REPARATION, COMPENSATIONS, OR MONETARY FORFEITURE OWING TO THE INFORMATION INCLUDED HEREIN, EITHER IN A DIRECT OR AN INDIRECT WAY.
LEGAL NOTICE: THIS BOOK HAS COPYRIGHT PROTECTION. YOU CAN USE THE BOOK FOR PERSONAL PURPOSE. YOU SHOULD NOT SELL, USE, ALTER, DISTRIBUTE, QUOTE, TAKE EXCERPTS OR PARAPHRASE IN PART OR WHOLE THE MATERIAL CONTAINED IN THIS BOOK WITHOUT OBTAINING THE PERMISSION OF THE AUTHOR FIRST. DISCLAIMER NOTICE: YOU MUST TAKE NOTE THAT THE INFORMATION IN THIS DOCUMENT IS FOR CASUAL READING AND ENTERTAINMENT PURPOSES ONLY. WE HAVE MADE EVERY ATTEMPT TO PROVIDE ACCURATE, UP TO DATE AND RELIABLE INFORMATION. WE DO NOT EXPRESS OR IMPLY GUARANTEES OF ANY KIND. THE PERSONS WHO READ ADMIT THAT THE WRITER IS NOT OCCUPIED IN GIVING LEGAL, FINANCIAL, MEDICAL OR OTHER ADVICE. WE PUT THIS BOOK CONTENT BY SOURCING VARIOUS PLACES. PLEASE CONSULT A LICENSED PROFESSIONAL BEFORE YOU TRY ANY TECHNIQUES SHOWN IN THIS BOOK. BY GOING THROUGH THIS DOCUMENT, THE BOOK LOVER COMES TO AN AGREEMENT THAT UNDER NO SITUATION IS THE AUTHOR ACCOUNTABLE FOR ANY FORFEITURE, DIRECT OR INDIRECT, WHICH THEY MAY INCUR BECAUSE OF THE USE OF MATERIAL CONTAINED IN THIS DOCUMENT, INCLUDING, BUT NOT LIMITED TO, – ERRORS, OMISSIONS, OR INACCURACIES.

ADVENTURES

TRAVEL IS CALLING

I POSSESS

THE FREEDOM TO TRAVEL

wherever I desire

TO TRAVEL
IS TO LIVE

TRAVEL
IS MY THERAPY

HOBBIES

HOBBIES HELP ME
STAND OUT
from the rest

RELAX AND ENJOY ACTIVITIES

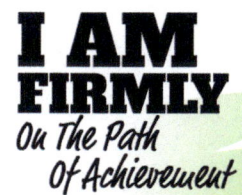

Achievements

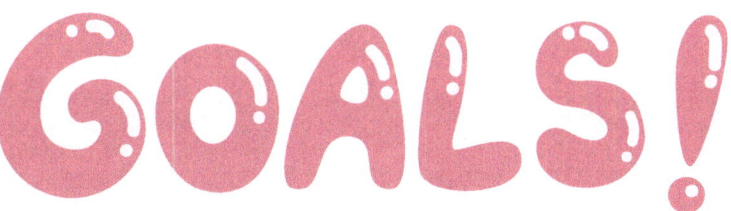

I CAN DO ANYTHING I SET MY MIND TO

SPIRITUALITY

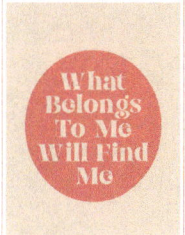

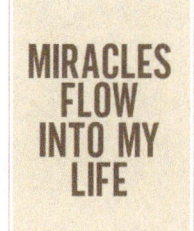
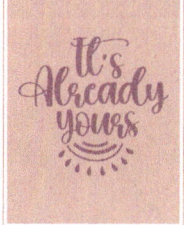

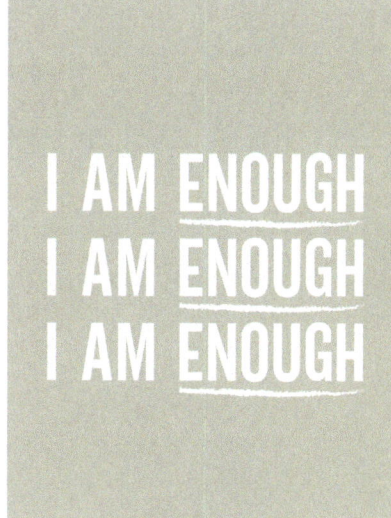

I AM ONE WITH ALL

LOVE IS MY PRIORITY

Relationship

I'm not addicted to COFFEE we are just in a very committed RELATIONSHIP

Distance means so little when Friendship means so much

Laughter & Friendship will cure just about ANYTHING

I DESERVE FULFILLING RELATIONSHIPS

I DESERVE

LOVE

AS I AM

dream together

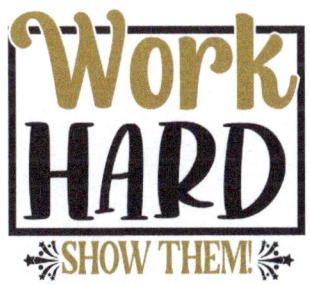   

MY BUSINESS ALLOWS ME TO HAVE A LIFE I LOVE

I CAN ACHIEVE ANY GOALS IN BUSINESS

this is us
OUR LIFE. OUR STORY. OUR HOME.

HOME

I DESERVE AN AMAZING HOME

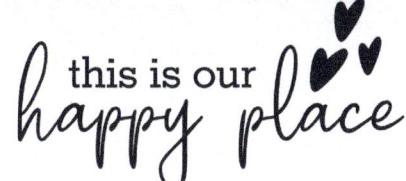
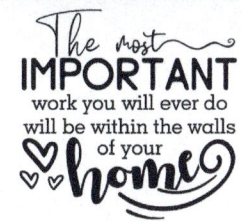

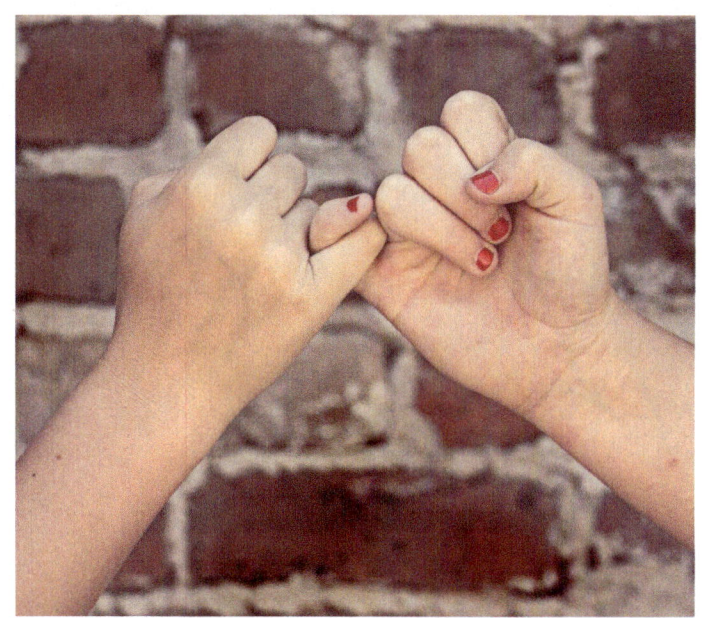

FRIENDS

 To have a friend and be a friend is what makes life worthwhile  Thank you for being my unpaid therapist #bestfriends

NOT SISTERS by blood BUT SISTERS BY Heart 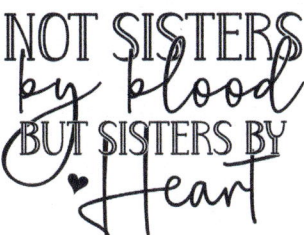  It's not what we have in life, but who we have that matters

I AM DEEPLY GRATEFUL FOR MY FRIENDS

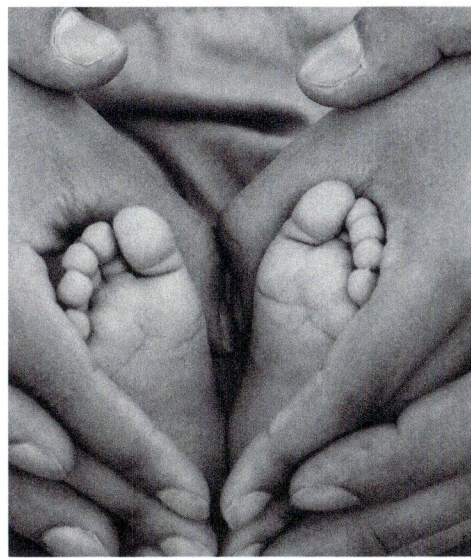

 **FAMILY**

You call it Chaos we call it Family

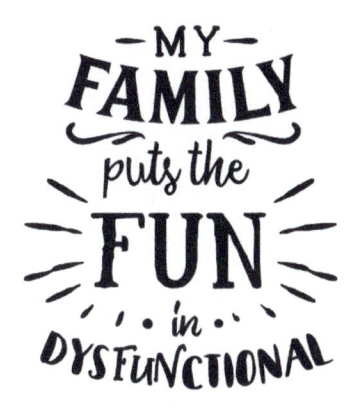

HOME is WHEREVER MY BUNCH OF crazies are

MY FAMILY puts the FUN in DYSFUNCTIONAL

YOU CALL IT CHAOS WE call it FAMILY

You are my SUN MY MOON and all of MY STARS

TOGETHER is our FAVORITE PLACE TO BE

WHEREVER THE FAMILY IS THAT'S home

the LOVE OF A FAMILY IS LIFE'S GREATEST BLESSING

HOME IS WHERE THE IS

family WHERE LIFE BEGINS & love never ENDS.

FAMILY MAKES THIS HOUSE A HOME

FAMILY WHERE LIFE BEGINS & love NEVER ENDS.

WE ARE UNITED IN OUR LOVE FOR ONE ANOTHER

Family WHERE LIFE BEGINS AND LOVE NEVER ENDS

SELF LOVE

GO GIRL!

SELFCARE

take care of your mind
BE KIND TO YOUR SELF
I AM THAT GIRL
be kind to yourself be kind to yourself
SELF-CARE
Self Care Comes First
SLEEP WELL
do what makes you happy
STAND UP!
DAILY DOSE OF VITAMIN D
I ENJOY TAKING CARE OF MYSELF
You are ENOUGH
Hydrate. Move. Sleep.
Self-care IS EMPOWERMENT
YOU ARE BEAUTIFUL
do it for you

MONEY ISN'T EVERYTHING BUT EVERYTHING NEED MONEY

talk **BUSINESS** *to me*

but first **CASH**

FINANCE

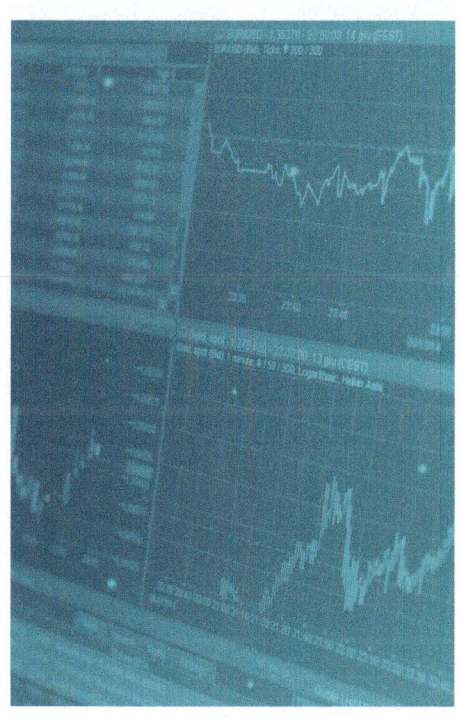

My success is inevitable

Empowered Women Empower Women

Behind every successful woman is herself

Waiting on rest DAY Excuses don't BURN Calories Running Late is my Cardio Fear is a Liar GYM hair don't Care Cardio is hardio

WORKOUT

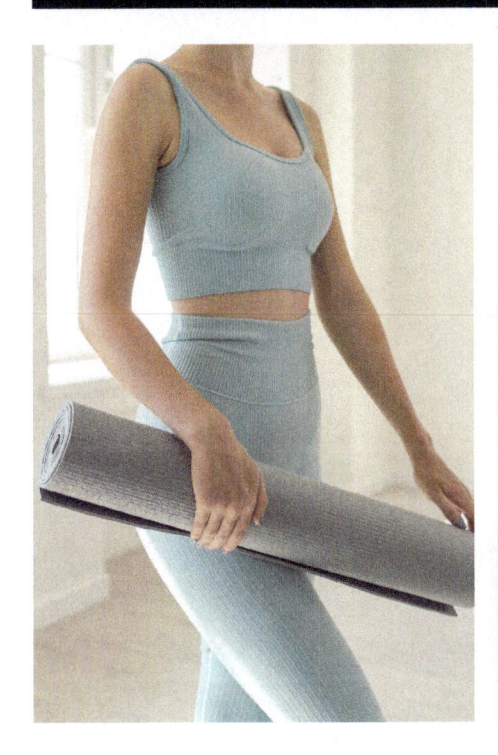

STAY ACTIVE!

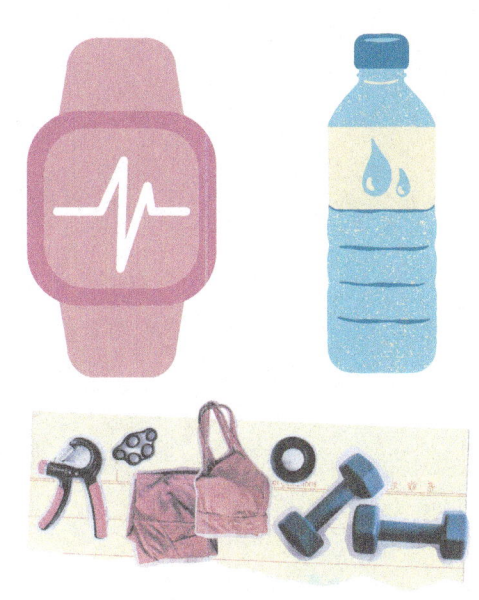

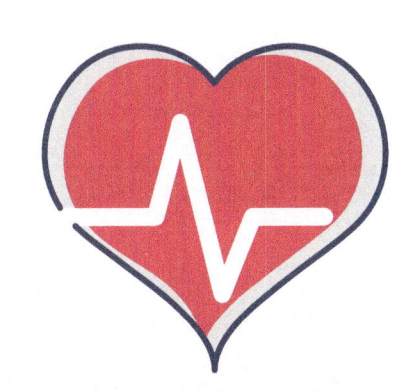

THE PAIN YOU FEEL TODAY WILL BE THE STRENGTH YOU FEEL TOMORROW

EXERCISE

TODAY

I AM FIT AND POWERFUL

GYM

IMPORTANT!

MAKE IT HAPPEN

HEALTHY EATING

Make yourself a priority

Eat HEALTHY live long LIVE Strong

Stay STRONG live LONG

a HEALTHY mind IN A HEALTHY BODY

ENERGIZE your LIFE

A healthy FUTURE begins now

Healthy food Healthy life

Health IS Wealth

My body is my friend and I treat it as such

I appreciate the instrument my body is

I EAT WELL AND FEEL GOOD IN MY BODY

healthy BODY healthy LIFE

I NEVER DREAMED ABOUT SUCCESS I Worked FOR IT

NEVER STOP WORKING

Work For A Cause Not For Applause

I have a plan*

Say Yes to new adventures

Work Hard Pray Harder

Work & Business

I NEVER DREAMED ABOUT SUCCESS I Worked FOR IT

idea

Prove yourself to yourself not others.

CREATIVE STARTUP

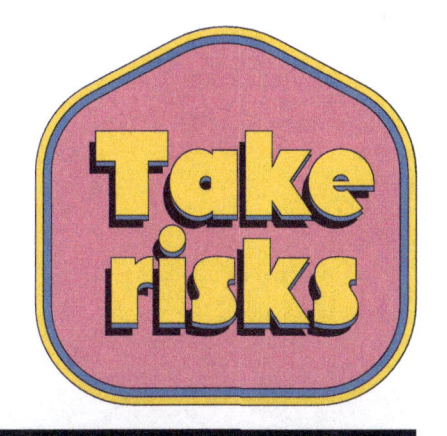

- WHO YOU ARE Tomorrow Begins With WHAT YOU DO today
- Use Your mistakes To Build STAIRS Not Walls
- I NEVER Dreamed ABOUT SUCCESS I Worked FOR IT
- Dreams Don't Work UNLESS You Do
- Great Job
- HARD WORK BEATS TALENT
- Take risks
- I AM MOTIVATED, CONSISTENT, AND DETERMINED
- you're 100!
- DON'T QUIT
- Nice JOB!
- Great Work
- you're one in a million
- YOU CAN!
- You Can Do ANYTHING

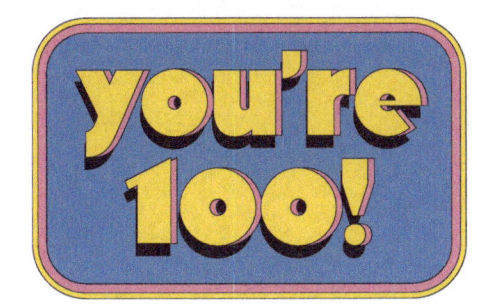

Bonus Elements

Believe in Yourself!

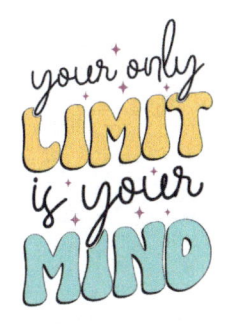

- Happy Mind / Happy Mind / Happy Mind / Happy Mind
- Be Kind
- Falling Down Is An Accident Staying Down Is A Today
- your only LIMIT is your MIND
- Self Love Club
- Start Today
- You Got This / You Got This / You Got This / You Got This
- Making Dreams Come True
- Dreams Don't Work Unless You Do
- Be Kind always
- Dream it wish it Do it
- you are living your STORY
- Choose Happy
- Never Quit Your Dreams
- It's Just A Bad Day Not A Bad Life
- Life is tough BUT SO AM I

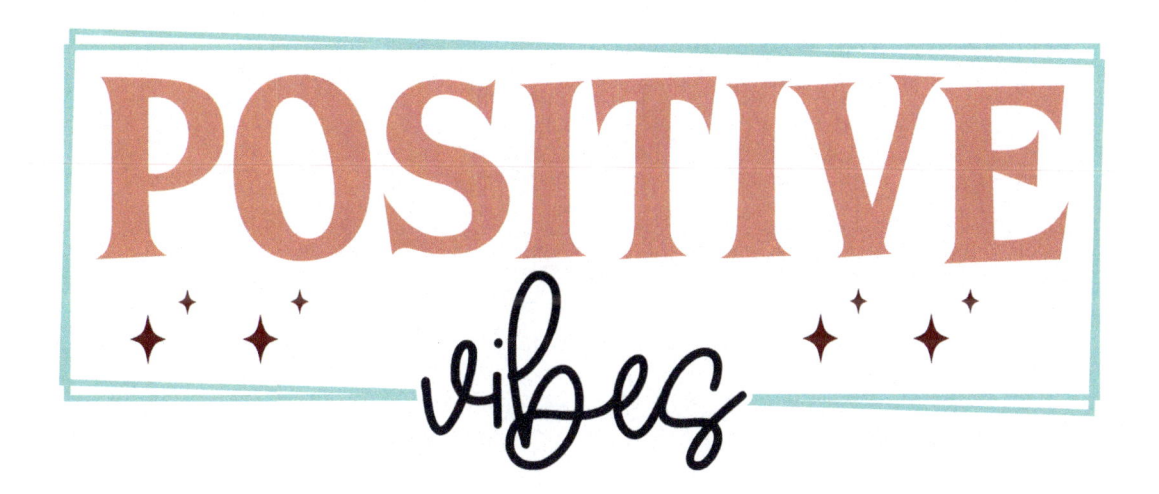

POSITIVE vibes

YOU TOTALLY GOT THIS

TOMORROW NEEDS YOU

SELF CARE IS NOT SELFISH

NO BAD DAYS
NO BAD DAYS
NO BAD DAYS
NO BAD DAYS

MENTAL HEALTH MATTERS

LIFE IS TOUGH BUT SO ARE YOU

GOD GIVES HIS HARDEST BATTLES TO HIS TOUGHEST SOLDIERS

HARD TIMES DO NOT LAST FOREVER

BRIGHTER DAYS AHEAD

BE REAL not perfect

Focus ON THE GOOD

MOTIVATIONAL

Striving to Be an esther

Striving to Be an esther

Saved by his AMAZING grace

Raising tiny disciples

Life is tough but so are you

LIFE IS FRAGILE HANDLE With Prayer

Just Livin the DREAM

She is STRONG Proverbs 31:25

- NEXT Month
- today
- to do
- NOTES
- DO IT
- YUP!
- WORKOUT
- next
- NO no
- don't forget
- GOALS
- do it
- WORKOUT
- yes
- THIS WEEK
- CHECK List

IT'S TIME TO PLAN

- NEXT
- YES
- NO
- tomorrow
- REMEMBER
- IMPORTANT
- CHECK List

Laugh & be happy

EMBRACE THE JOY OF LIFE

20 ♥ 24

HELLO 2024

Thank you!

We are thrilled to extend our heartfelt gratitude for your recent purchase of our **Vision Board Clip Art Book for 2024**. Your support means the world to us, and we can't wait for you to explore the creative possibilities that await within its pages.

We believe that creating a vision board is an incredible journey towards manifesting your dreams and goals. With this clip art book, we aimed to provide you with a toolkit to make that journey even more exciting and visually engaging. We trust that the vibrant illustrations and versatile elements will empower your vision board to truly reflect your aspirations.

As you dive into your creative projects, we kindly request your feedback. Your thoughts are invaluable to us and to others who are considering enhancing their creative process with our book. If you have a moment to spare, we would greatly appreciate it if you could share your experience and insights in a few words on Amazon. Your honest review will help fellow dreamers make informed decisions and discover the magic of our **Vision Board Clip Art Book.**

Wishing you endless inspiration and success as you craft your vision board masterpiece in 2024!

Warm regards,
Jasmine Eason

Printed in Great Britain
by Amazon